The Office Administrator's Handbook For 'Super Efficiency'

Kenneth Cartwright(B.Ed.Hons) Business

The Office Administrator's Handbook For 'Super Efficiency'

Core Information-Free Offers-Evaluation DVD at: www.intreps.co.uk

To Suit Who?

All of the following will discover value in this hand-book:
- Urgent Job Seekers
- Sole Business Proprietors
- Small Business Proprietors
- Business Students
- Unofficial Business Auditors

Urgent Job Seekers:

By applying the information contained in this book,
entry possibilities into the world of business administration
are boosted phenomenally, through:
- The acquisition of specialised knowledge,
- facilitating:
  - The efficient use of the best trade tools for the job
  - The adoption of proven efficiency methods, for operational speed and reliability
  - The easy-rapid production of 'auto-generated' enhanced outputs
- The acquisition and the usage of reliable low-overhead computer software tools, adaptable for any working scenario

In the context of the above points, persons not previously trained and without previous experience will – given the opportunity – confidently improve any working scenario, in terms of:
- Speed of operations
- Accuracy and/or reliability
- Quality of outputs
- The establishment and/or the improvement of collaboration facilities, widespread within their organisation

Job Interviewees who have fully utilised this book, and who have progressed themselves in practice/efficiency terms will always impress and surprise their interviewers, by means of their acquired ICT resources and their acquired specialised knowledge/skills. Given trial opportunities, they will always succeed impressively. Given real employment opportunities, they will always lead the way.

Sole Business Proprietors:

Tradesmen operating unilaterally with insufficient time/knowledge/experience to complete their day-to-day office work, will discover the means to facilitate untrained supporters, without necessary dependence on external specialists. In this context, they will be able to significantly reduce their administrative overheads. Where they choose to expand, they will also gain the means to facilitate untrained employees/trainees, to operate with efficiency and reliability at low cost.

Small Business Proprietors:

This book will maximise all efforts in the business office, in terms of time, efficiency and quality. In this context – with much time saved – unwilling office administrators will gain time to return to the shop floor/workshop etc. Conversely, willing administrators will gain significant time opportunities for development/improvement.

Business Students:

By means of this book, all of the fodder that is fed to business students in schools and colleges, is significantly augmented with 'real' practical facilitation. Where 95% of business lecturers in schools and colleges do not possess 'real' business experience, this augmentation is much more valuable to prospective employers, than certificates and/or limited work experience. Also, because the framework of NVQ(National Vocational Qualifications) is devised within conventional boundaries, the value of this book also exceeds NVQ validations.

Unofficial Business Auditors:

Business managers who ordinarily do not possess specific office operations knowledge/skills, who wish to investigate accuracy and/or efficiency aspects within their domains, will be able to acquire such, by means of this book.

Tools For The Trade

Base Skills:

Keyboard Operations:

'Touch Typing' – no looking – keyboard skills remain extremely valuable within 'all' contemporary business scenes, even with the arrival of touch-screen technology. Still, the input of masses of alpha characters remains, as the biggest hindrance to business administration operations, World-wide, even in the wake of voice recognition developments. In this context, properly proficient keyboard operators are very valuable, when they work at maximum efficiency. Nowadays, such efficiency is dependent on computer hardware(for physical input) and software(for manipulation). Where self-taught operators usually end up being the best, specialised keyboard training software removes unnecessary difficulties and/or obstacles. Specific advice about this is obtainable through the 'Contact INTREPs' link at www.intreps.co.uk.

Language:

Basic English language and specialised 'Technical Authorship' competences are possessed by the author, who is reachable through the 'Contact INTREPs' link at www.intreps.co.uk. Appropriate training remains available, on request.

Numeracy:

Abilities to 'number crunch' are improved significantly by undertaking INTREPs 'Mod 4 Extras' – ECDL styled - MS Excel training. Information about this training is obtained at www.intreps.co.uk at the 'Training' link. Additional information is also obtained at the 'Contact INTREPs' link at www.intreps.co.uk.

Computer Hardware:

After decades of software 'push', the hardware scene has finally arrived. Portable units possessing all that is required for reliable and efficient inter-action(inter communication with Bluetooth and Wi-Fi). Operating instantaneously when properly maintained, all are now available at very low cost. In relation to office operations, with Microsoft churning out 'big overhead' system software(MS Windows) for years and years, all was a travesty since the launch of MS Windows 95. Then, users were manically upgrading RAM like beavers. Shrewd operators then, adopted the strategy of running outdated – tried and tested - legacy software on new hardware. In this way high-speed operations were ensured without much care about the successive 'upgrade' phenomenon, much concocted by software houses, in particular, Microsoft. The nerds that pre-occupied themselves with running the latest software, rarely understand business constraints and efficiency essentials, and least of all do they comprehend the difficulties of the glorious upgrade caper. Most sensible businesses stick to the old software for a long time, to avoid all of the staff retraining nightmares. Thus, 'run old software on new machines' is now an established convention.

On the laptop front, a number of problems have arisen however. The infamous IBM track-point disappeared because of design difficulties. It could not be manufactured to function reliably, but for artisan keyboard operators it was the panacea of ease and speed. Always in the midst of spread fingers working instinctively. Now, alternative finger-touch pointing devices frequently run wild with hands and wrist stretched over them. Real keyboard artisans – those that can navigate around a keyboard without looking, quickly and efficiently – are often tempted to switch the damned pointing device off: more a hindrance than a help. For all of the new touch-screen trend, the keyboard remains as the master tool for rapid/efficient operations. Yet, manufacturers have now 'swinged' on this. In a cost cutting fervour, they have stopped providing spring loaded keys that respond to distinctive finger pressure. Contemporary keyboards are now arrays of button pads, not much indicative of pressure or movement. Really a touch typist's nightmare, and a copy typist's quagmire of duplication and triplication, sometimes. The only sensible thing to appear out of the new 'wide-screen' trend, is the incorporation of a convenient number pad, which is essential for number crunching operators. Not really a revelation though, because plug-in USB number pads have been available for a long time now. In all, the biggest boost achieved with new hardware is Wi-Fi, for flexible networking: undoubtedly.

Computer Interface Uniformity:

If computer networking is the panacea of flexibility and convenience, then all is somewhat rendered impotent with the prevalence of 'system software' and 'application software' version variations. Truly the 'screw-up' phenomenon of the decade, with Microsoft continuously launching new versions, almost year by year. With operating systems pre-installed on new machines universally nowadays, varied multi-user environments – with mixes of old/new machines – inhibit user utilisation between machines rather drastically. Moreso, where uniformity is vigorously pursued – with old machines being upgraded to the latest versions – staff are regularly forced to revise their user skills, much to the distraction of their day-to-day functions. Even competence attestation with the use of Microsoft self-testing software(ITEC testing) has become worthless, due to the non-accommodation of 'hot key operations'. Those in the know eagerly use 'hot-key' actions because – within MS Office especially – they function properly within all versions. A jump between MS Vista and MS Windows 7 is daunting, but it remains plausible within the forfeiture of a mornings' work time. A jump between MS Office 2003 and MS Office 2010 is however, beyond grasping distance within the forfeiture of a weeks' work. Who is in a position to afford all of this?

If 'knowledge' is power, then business managers gain immense power with just a small amount of knowledge, relating to the easy achievement of computerised 'uniformity'. It is not only possible, but absolutely feasible to run all sorts of computers – with various operating systems and with differentiated on-board application software – within a single styled user interface, with identical application software on all machines, with each efficiently inter-connected. The era of virtualisation is here. With the increased capability of hardware nowadays, users can easily switch between a new gismo machine running the latest OS and the latest application software, and MS Windows XP, to use MS Office 2003. More particularly, they can share any sort of tried and tested utility/amenity uniformly. Where these are old-styled legacy software applications, they run faster, anyway. Above all, prudent managers steer away from expensive over-rated contemporary software, which most often, is BETA untried. In this context, the 'avoid unsupported facilities' argument is nullified. Support is invariably required for novices, whereas, long-standing computer usage produces experts.

For further information about achieving user interface uniformity, use the 'Contact INTREPs' link at www.intreps.co.uk.

MS Office:

Broad skill development:

In the context of Microsoft Office, Sun Microsystem's 'Open Office' is somewhat primitive, particularly the database partition. It might be free, but you only get what you pay for, is a true dictum in this case. Where it is used, extensive usage capability is sacrificed. Where often, only 10% of Microsoft Office's true capabilities are conventionally utilised in the workplace, many so-called experienced users are surprisingly enlightened – big-time – with the completion of ECDL(European Computer Driving Licence) styled training, comprising 7 main modules, each of which take a day to complete within a conventional classroom scenario. It is feasible and practical however to flexibly complete this training on a 'distance tuition' basis, within a one-to-one scenario. Check this out at www.intreps.co.uk.

Managing lots of specialised data:

A lot of proprietary application software – such as 'Synchro' for foundries, 'Ford' for car dealers and 'Garage Manager' for car service depots – has been produced by small software houses, using Microsoft's Visual Basic to produce locked front-end facilities, which are actually fed – openly – from MS Access data tables. With a view to fixing inherent problems with these applications, basic MS Office users can be progressed rapidly and effectively into the 'expert' realm of MS Access operations and configurations, by means of specific distance tuition, through from 'basic' – within ECDL styled training – to 'intermediate', providing for relational database innovations to quite a competent level. Additionally, special 'See-It', 'Copy-It', 'Do-It' styled distance tuition potentially progresses users to 'expert' MS Access configuration levels. Importantly though, where staff skill development is not pursued, a stock range of existing MS Access utility applications – all of which run automatically within MS Office – is available for immediate implementation. Where MS Access user skills have been developed, and where an existing stock utility has been implemented, scope for locally implemented 'integrated extensions' becomes available. Check out: MS Office 'Additions' and 'Intermediate Database Training' at www.intreps.co.uk.

Simple 'Web' authoring:

Web pages can be created within MS Office, very rapidly and very easily. Integrated facilities exist to rapidly convert hard-copy documents – with graphics – into this form. All of which can be augmented and/or amended and Intranet published with lightning speed. Additionally, the following are completed with ease:

  i. MS Access/MS Excel dynamic data linking
  ii. MS Access/MS Word dynamic data linking
  iii. Active web pages – Intranet
  iv. Active web pages - Internet

For further information, use the 'Contact INTREPs' link at www.intreps.co.uk.

Book-Keeping Training:

Who Wants To Utilise BK Training?:
  1. Willing office administration personnel:
      a. For employment progression - improving skills/capabilities – which will increase employment worth and work status
      b. For work scope expansion in pursuit of new challenges. Thus to diminish monotony and employment ruts
  2. Sole Proprietor and Partnership Employers:
      a. To achieve vertical business integration without employing extra specialists. Thus, providing existing enthusiastic staff with progression opportunities
      b. To achieve self-audit capabilities, in terms of being able to check the output quality of external providers

Willing office workers with adequate basic numeracy skills, but without 'Financial Control' knowledge can be trained to impressive proficiency levels within very short periods, by means of clever training tactics. Such tactics make use of special computer software that virtually self-trains learners by permitting the mis-posting of transactions which detrimentally distort final statements. Importantly, this software also permits detail and values alterations – not permitted by conventional financial control software – to achieve corrections. With the training tool sorted, the tactical training approach progresses learners by feeding them with typical day-to-day styled 'Sole Proprietor' and 'Partnership' financial fodder, all to be summarised within MS Excel, in the form of 'End of Period' statements. Of course, the transaction posting software sends all of its incorporated data to MS Excel automatically in detail and in summary, much to facilitate the production of scrolling analysis lists and 'End of Period' statements.

Further information is obtained by means of the 'Book-Keeping' training link at www.intreps.co.uk and at the 'Contact INTREPs' link at the same web site.

Advanced Computerised Accounting Training:

Who Wants To Utilise ACA Training?:

1. Business managers – short of staff with high-end computer skills - faced with laborious record keeping tasks: Typically, the monthly production of management accounts, regular costs analysis, VAT Intrastat documentation and all sorts of other 'essential' routines

2. Business proprietors and business managers seeking essential analysis information, in order to increase business efficiency. Typically:
   a. Tight stock control by means of accurate forecasting

b. Automatic workshop/shop floor data input for front office analysis, much to facilitate efficient purchase ordering

What is really being talked about here, is the fostering of MS Office skills to the level of VBA(Visual Basic for Applications) manipulation, which flexibly provides for MS Office application 'automation'. The utilisation/adaptation of pre-developed utilities and the development of new utilities to complete the automatic performance of regular – laborious – routines, which are customarily labour intensive. For example, MS Excel is configured to grab detailed data from day-to-day book-keeping ledgers, to produce departmental management accounts, for manager/director business analysis, fully automatically. In this way, at the end of each working month, the required documentation is produced within ten minutes. When otherwise performed manually, this process typically consumes an accountant's time for a whole working week.

Further information is obtained by means of the 'ACA' training link at www.intreps.co.uk and at the 'Contact INTREPs' link at the same web site.

Computerised Graphics Processing Training:

Business 'High-Quality' Graphics:

Who Needs To Produce Them?:
1. All who are not professionally geared, not wishing to buy-in specific specialists:
   a. Photographers
   b. Graphic artists
   c. Publishers: brochures, catalogues, fly-sheets

Where digitisation has done much to minimise essential image capturing skills, an awful lot of 'mis-information' is about nowadays about the best computer software for the job. Much to contradict all of the hype about 'Adobe Photoshop', a suitable – single - universally capable computer application is not available for business people, wishing to obtain high quality results, with speed and ease. Yet, astounding results are consistently achievable with 'speed' and 'ease', by means of the best features of a number of old legacy graphic applications. All of which, operate very rapidly on modern platforms. Typically, these unique software features:
1. Provide directly for scanned captures
2. Provide for the identification and the organisation of images, as to:
   a. Rapid thumbnail production
   b. Moving, duplicating, deleting with linked file/folder management
   c. Accurate re-sizing and print sizing
   d. Controlling inter-polation and compression ratios
   e. Changing file formats
   f. Renditioning, as to Saturation, Contrast, Brightness, Gamma
   g. Captioning – using the incumbent MS Windows font range

h. Cropping: internal and external
i. Red-eye removal
j. GIF animation viewing and creations
k. 3D Titling
l. Blemish removal
m. Multiple image integration/placement/management
n. Auto image masking with corresponding back-filling – with multiple graduation features

With all of the appropriate legacy software FOC(Free of Charge) and licence free, the only requirements for the exploitation of available facilities are:

1. Conventional low-tech hardware
2. Incumbent personnel willing to venture
3. Appropriate 'Know-How'

To acquire the described software and the appropriate 'Know-How', use the 'Computer Graphics Training' link at www.intreps.co.uk and/or the 'Contact INTREPs' link at the same web site.

In The Shadow Of The World-Wide-Web Market Place

Getting Out There:

At the most primitive level, Sole Proprietor/Partnership businesses establish a www presence by:

1. Contracting with an ISP(Internet Service Provider) for:
   a. A unique domain name
   b. Web storage space on the ISP's server/servers. 'www.GoDaddy.com' currently provides these for just £1.00 per month.
2. Acquiring an appropriate FTP(File Transfer Protocol) computer application, and configuring it to connect to the specified web storage space
3. Uploading suitable web pages to the specified web storage space. When the www browsing public enter the appropriate URL(uniform resource locator) in the form of www.name(domain name).co.uk/com/org/tv etc into the address window of their browser, the home page at this location is displayed

As already mentioned, the appropriate web pages can be created within MS Word/Excel/PowerPoint with speed and ease, but unfortunately – beyond the MS Office 97 version – they cannot be re-edited with anything other than MS Office – of the same version – with any sort of convenience, due to the complexity of the incumbent code. Worse, versions of MS Office later than 97, frequently render page contents inaccurately in the initial document birth process, much to the frustration of many 'Office' users. In opposition to the revelations of many 'Adobe DreamWeaver' suit enthusiasts, the most viable expedient of web page creation is definitely not the utilisation of proprietary software such as 'DreamWeaver', because this functions much to the same style of MS Office. It provides a 'Word Processing' interface, which automatically converts all of the incorporated ASCII content into web code(html, dtml, xml etc, depending on the software version). It is all a bit like getting a handyman to paint your garden fence, instead of doing it yourself. Invariably, you end up stating: "No, I meant the other way, or the other thing, or the other colour", or "You have used the wrong colour, or the wrong brand". Without direct control, absolute control is lost. Anyway, with all of the incumbent over-complicated – over laborious – code, proprietary software produced web pages function much slower than need be. Most often however, where complicated functionality is required – https security for transaction processing in particular – they have to be used. Yet most are not able to completely provide viable solutions in total, such as functional *server-sided scripts for reliable data input from browsing end users. There are exceptions to this assumption. Old-styled legacy software – using pure html – remains very functional for the production of 'Product Catalogues', running rapidly, providing product organisation, with viewers much assisted in their dissemination activities. Specific one-to-one distance training also remains available for the use of this software, along with a number of cranky old utilities that do things, not done by any of the so-called modern wonder tools. For example, old-styled GIF graphics animation utilities that are very quick and easy to use with just a little bit of common sense, or screen image grabbing utilities – either 'still' or 'video' – that accurately discriminate, as opposed to just grabbing all of the screen or just active windows.

* Server Sided: scripts that run at web servers in response to requests from client sided scripts

Reliable Web Outputs For Sole Proprietor and Partnership Businesses

For the production of web pages that appear as originally intended, at speed, creators have to get to grips with source code, which at fundamental level is HTML version 4, at least. This is used either as in its pure form to host ASCII text and JPG/GIF graphics, or as a shell host to other complementary codes: Java script or applets, DTML, XML, CGI, PHP etc. The cleverest, the simplest and the most reliable method of creating www web pages, is to manually create/edit HTML source code, within which it is most often, feasible and practical to embed copy/paste tried and tested portions of PHP or CGI or Java applets, or whatever else. In this way, absolute control over appearance and functionality – with a lot of speed – is maintained. For those that shout: "Oh, it is all so laborious", the availability of licence free 'semi-coding' web applications is emphasised here. Within these, code turns red when a defect exists, just like 'Pascal' or 'Visual Basic'. The code for tables/lists is generated automatically, and because the user's mind is on code – not on word processing – it is easily verifiable; even tweaked further when necessary – as soon as it is posted to the working page. When combining the efficient FIND feature and the MS Windows 'Clipboard', all of the incorporated hyperlinks are altered successively in a jiff with CNTRL/F and CNTRL/V. Similarly, all common tags – after an initial copy action – are inserted with amazing rapidity. Also, with this sort of application, when a tag composition has been forgotten, users are rapidly reminded with a direct reference list, and so on. All just requires a bit of 'Know-How' coupled with elements of personal organisation.

To acquire the described software and the appropriate 'Know-How', use the 'HTML Training' link at www.intreps.co.uk and/or the 'Contact INTREPs' link at the same web site.

20

The Data Storing Syndrome

Who Needs 'Specialised' Data Storing Facilities?:

All businesses! The common problem has been to-date, that
most office administrators – commonly using MS Excel frequently
– have assumed that MS Excel is the most suitable application for
this purpose, but in reality, although it features some
DB(database) facilities, it is not much use beyond the retention of
'flat-file' arrays of data, most often manually appended with a
great deal of laboriousness. Repetitive posting is required in the
absence of automatic pick-post features. Much disregarding the
most important principle of efficient data storing: the avoidance of
repetitive data entry.

Who Needs DB Training?:

In relation to office administrators, most 'so-called' experienced
users end up improving their user skills with the completion of
ECDL Module 6 – Database styled training. By means of this,
learners begin to grasp the concept of data 'relationships', much
applying this with the assistance of notorious Microsoft 'Wizards'.
Yet real appreciation of the enormous capabilities of MS Access –
and even moreso within Microsoft SQL Server – is achieved with
guidance away from 'Wizards', and with the utilisation – within
training scenarios – of clever DB examples that absolutely control
data-entry users, making data duplication, wrong data entry and
incomplete records, absolutely impossible. All is really about
preserving data quality for the facilitation of efficient and reliable
information production, for management decision making. For
example, after a particular vehicle has been booked out of a DB
transport control utility, it should not then be available for pick-
post 'booking out' until it has been booked-in again. Extended
training beyond ECDL – which is usually completed within short
time spans on a one-to-one distance tuition basis – fosters

'parent/child' structured data storage, within strictly controlled user interfaces, appearing and disappearing automatically in accordance with user operations. Extending these principles, training concepts place individual DBs as inter-linked modules within extended DBMSs(Database Management Systems), with virgin data being posted only once, ever. For example typically, employee payroll records are automatically passed through to workshop work records. Additionally, car stock control records – along with employee payroll records - are automatically passed through to car sales records. All is about reducing the need for duplicated data entry, but with 'pick-posting' facilities, all is also about data entry accuracy. Additionally, modular approaches provide for flexibility and for expansion in the context of future proofing.

In fact, the modular DB approach is extraordinarily powerful when it is pursued to the extreme, with the use of a 'principal' source data module, from which all child modules acquire their related data fully automatically. Working with 'event histories' – with the utilisation of defaulted dates and times – this amenity is valuable to all business types. It stores:

1. Employees: with the inclusion of:
   a. Important work completed
   b. Personal strengths/weaknesses
   c. Particular working restrictions
2. Suppliers
3. Customers: with the inclusion of:
   a. A history of contacts
   b. A history of purchases
4. Projects: with the inclusion of:
   a. Involved employees
   b. All relevant documentation storage locations
   c. Work schedules
   d. Specifications
   e. Completed meetings

f. Proposed meetings
5. Equipment/Machinery: with the inclusion of:
a. Delivery dates
b. Service schedules
c. Warranty information
d. Pertinent service facilitators

Thus, database – or DBMS – creation training is best conducted within range of this 'Core' DB module, which is easily network shared between all relevant business departments, either as a 'Client' MS Access database for flexible data-entry, or as a reference Intranet web page, which of course is automatically updated in response to data appendages/amendments. Typically, the Core DB module – as described – forms the crux of 'Call Centre' day-to-day operations, storing automatically date and time stamped – history styled – records of each and every human contact that occurs, ad-infinitum. In this way, 'stories' of everything – for everybody and everything – evolve to facilitate action responses, scheduled or otherwise. Where 'Parent'/Child' record relations are established automatically, the 'Parent/Child' or the 'Mother/Daughter' concept is expanded much further, merely by means of clever user data postings. For example: a 'Mother' project record which houses numerous 'Employee' identities - used for the allocation and the completion of tasks – is in turn, related to 'Employee Details' records, held in a connected DBMS module.

For further information about this, use the 'INTREPs Prospects' link at www.intreps.co.uk. For further information about ECDL styled database training, and for DB Intermediate Training use the 'Training' link at the same web site.

The Higher Echelons of Data Storage and Data Manipulation

Processing Volume Data:

Beyond the 'Intermediate' DB training level, even with the creation of suitable MS Office/Access – or MS SQL Server – facilities, existing data perhaps consequent of a long business history, is to be transferred into the new facility. This may have been previously stored in an old-styled flat-file type of database, or at worst, it is still in hard copy form. Drastically, maybe stored in a Kalamazoo styled card indexed system: masses of it. Previously, an agency has been used to recruit casual data-entry operators, to manually transfer from the old to the new. A very slow, laborious and expensive process. To be avoided if possible. Even with hard copies, OCR scanning is available within MS Office, to facilitate the creation of digitised data arrays, then easily and rapidly swallowed by MS Access, without keyboard operation requirements. Text exports from old flat-file DBs or word processors are made to house themselves within MS Access in the same way, after 'Formalisation' processes have been completed adequately. With just a little bit of 'Know-How' transfer which has been structurally pre-prepared within a specified training module, incumbent office administrators avoid most of the hidden difficulties of volume data entry. For further information use the 'Training' link at www.intreps.co.uk.

MS Access Final Outputs:

Of all of the virtues of MS Access – in total contrast to Open Office – the reporting features are the best, of all existing computer database applications, with the exception of MS SQL Server. Yet, in the wrong hands, they can also be sophisticated monsters. The art and skill of MS Access report preparations is a speciality in itself. Yet, this is not all of it. All or some of the contents of MS Access reports can be directly inserted into MS Word and MS Excel documents, without copy/paste operations, either by means of DDE(Dynamic Data Exchange) or by means of 'Office Links'. Rapid, efficient and easy, even for novice MS Office users, after all has been suitably configured. Additionally, where suitable web serving facilities have been pre-configured, the underlying data of MS Access reports is vended in web page form automatically with the use of MS Access 'Active Pages', which can feature sophisticated data filtering. Within these, even additional data-entry facilities are configurable. For further information use the 'Training' link at www.intreps.co.uk.

WWW & Intranet Web Publishing:

<u>Within New Intranets:</u>
Really, wide ranging Web Publishing abilities/skills are acquired progressively, firstly with the completion of:
1. HTML code authoring training
2. Computerised Graphics Processing training
3. MS Access Final Outputs training
4. SQL operations training

Then with the completion of broad-based Web Publishing training which pre-supposes competence as to the four training modules itemised above. In a consequent progressive fashion, this fosters the following knowledge/competences:
1. Features of MS Office applications, available as web page components
2. Automatic code generated by MS Front Page, for possible web page adaptations
3. Digital graphics processing utilities, available for the production of web graphics: panoramas, GIF animations, 3D Titling, Navigation buttons, DTML menus and Internet operational graphic-styled catalogues
4. Inter-Active Web Page CGI Scripting, for submission form provisions
5. SQL(Structured Querying Language) operations, to facilitate SQL code embedding within PHP web pages, residing on the Internet, connected to MS Access – or MySQL – databases. Also, to facilitate SQL command line operations within industry standard DBMSs
6. Apache Web Server and IIS(MS Internet Information Services) configurations, within LAN, WAN and Internet environs

<u>Within The Internet:</u>

All is about enticing and facilitating consumers, particularly within the modern Internet market by means of a functionally efficient www presence which can be flexibly amended/appended in response to the ever-changing world. In this context, all of the training described much eliminates dependence on – not so reliable – external specialists. Additionally, with the use of old-styled legacy software – much augmented with MS Office – the whole of the digital infrastructure is maintained, expanded and/or modified rapidly and easily because principally, it is not over complicated or over laborious, and because related originators/maintainers possess adequate knowledge and solid skills.

Facilities For Higher Level Business ICT Learning – 'See-It', 'Copy-It', 'Do-It'

Of all that is available to potential 'super' business administrators and business managers, 'See-It', 'Copy-It', 'Do-It' learning concepts are the jewel in the crown. Where it is pointless to re-invent the wheel, ranges of solutions to prevailing business administration problems already exist within the bounds of www.intreps.co.uk. Refer to INTREPs MS Office 'Additions' at www.intreps.co.uk for commercial database examples. Typically, where – tried and tested - INTREPs 'Work-Fact' exists to increase the operational efficiency of 'Workshops', its features are cleverly exploited for MS Access innovation training with the removal of one of its critical modules, to be replaced within the learning scene, by novice innovators. Learners get to witness full functionality by means of demonstrations – achieved by means of video animations within the distance learning scenario – and thus, they see all of the ideal interfaces. Additionally, they are supplied all but one of 'Work-Fact's' modules, with provisions to investigate back-end constructions and configurations. Having previously developed themselves to a high level of MS Access competence, they then have to fill the void to achieve the full functionality of all that has been provided. Thus, they gain opportunities to innovate unilaterally, by whatever means other than plagiarising. On completion, innovations are reviewed/tested by the tutor, with pertinent appraisals. Then most importantly, the new innovators gain comparison opportunities, between their own efforts, and those incorporated into the original.

This theme of training is conducive to the significant evolvement of creativity and innovation impetus, much to be valued within small to medium sized pioneering businesses, often in much need of improvement. Importantly, the concept so described is easily extended away from database innovation, in all sorts of directions: eg, web sites with missing pages, MS Word/Excel auto-operations documents with sections of VBA code missing etc. The provisions for such, can all emanate from www.intreps.co.uk.